WE WANT YOU HERE

THOM S. RAINER

B&H
PUBLISHING GROUP

NASHVILLE, TENNESSEE

978-1-4627-8089-1

Published by B&H Publishing Group
Nashville, Tennessee

Dewey Decimal Classification: 254.5
Subject Heading: CHURCH FELLOWSHIP \
FRIENDSHIP \ CHURCH

2 3 4 5 6 7 8 • 22 21 20 19 18

To

You who honored our church with your visit.

We are glad you came.

CONTENTS

ABOUT THE BOOK

I get it. Many of you who read this will think, *I don't think this was the guy we heard preach last Sunday—was it?* No, you are not crazy. I am not the local church pastor in your community. But I am connected to the church you visited.

First, if you are a follower of Jesus, we are all connected. Local churches in Annapolis, East Africa, Australia, and Antarctica—we share a bond and common mission through the gospel. We are all connected through Christ.

Second, I lead an online community of pastors who care about you deeply. I create content to help pastors in many different ways, but some time ago, a particular topic stuck a chord. I learned that the pastors in our online community are very concerned about finding the most effective way to say to guests who visit their church (and those who they hope will visit their church in the future), "We want you here." So I wrote this book as a way to help those of us who care about church guests.

I was in your shoes once. I know what it is like to join a new church community. I hope you will find help in the pages ahead. Because we *really* want you here.

Thom S. Rainer

CHAPTER 1

WE REALLY WANT YOU HERE

Thank you.

We know. Those two words can seem trivial. We say them so often we can take them for granted.

But we really do want to thank you for being a guest at our church. We do not take your visit lightly. You have given of your time and energy to come to our church.

So, thank you again. We really mean it.

You may have some questions about our church. You may have some questions about your experience when you visited.

We get it.

Anytime you go to a new place, there may be uncertainty, and there may be questions. Our staff and church leaders are available to help you. We want to be as transparent as possible. We want to tell you about our church. We want to hear from you. And we want to answer your questions. Please let us know how we can help.

We want you to know something else: We really want you here!

Okay, that may sound absurd on the surface. How can we really want you here unless we know you well? Let us share five key reasons and you may get a better idea of our excitement about your visit.

REASON #1: WE WANT YOU TO EXPERIENCE THE LOVE OF CHRIST.

We believe in Jesus Christ.

We believe he is the Savior of the world.

That is why we gather and worship at this church. Quite frankly, that is why we do what we do.

There are many good organizations out there. And many of them are doing a great job serving others and helping others. We are grateful for those organizations.

But churches are different. We do all we do because we love Christ. We know his love. We have experienced his love. We have given our lives to him.

You may already be a Christian. That is great. We hope that you can continue to experience the love of Christ at this church. Serving and loving Christ was never meant to be a solo effort. It was meant to be shared with fellow believers.

Maybe you aren't a Christian. Or maybe you have questions or doubts about being a Christian. We will explore this matter further in chapters 5 and 7. But please understand you are welcome here regardless. We want you to experience the love of Christ.

It is transforming.

It is forgiving.

It is life-changing.

Perhaps this reason is the greatest reason we are glad you are here. We really hope you experience the love of Christ at our church.

Nothing could be more important.

REASON #2: WE WANT TO SERVE YOU.

Everyone has needs. Everyone has hurts at points in his or her life. Everyone has questions too.

We really love serving people and meeting needs. We would really love to serve you.

What is your need? Do you have questions about marriage, children, and family? Have you experienced the pain of loss in recent months? Do you feel lonely at times?

We want to serve you.

You will find at our church a number of people who find it a great joy to serve others. Many of them may have walked in your shoes. Someone in this church had experiences amazingly close to yours.

You may feel like you don't want to bother us. Hear us clearly. We take great joy in serving others, in serving you. So please, don't hesitate to tell one of us how we can help you. Please let us know. Don't think for a moment you are alone. We are with you and for you.

But you may not be experiencing some tough moments at this point in your life. We know that life has peaks and valleys. You may not be experiencing those lower moments right now. Instead, you came to this church to see if it is a place where you can connect and where you can make a difference.

That is another reason we really want you here.

REASON #3: WE WANT YOU TO MAKE A DIFFERENCE.

Frances Mason was her name. She lived to be almost ninety years old, and she made every day count. She loved her church. And she loved people.

Frances had this never-ending desire to make a difference for God. And she had two primary passions. First, she had the passion to pray. Rarely will you see someone so committed to prayer. Second, she had this crazy notion that God designed everyone to make a difference.

Okay, it's not such a crazy notion.

Frances knew that, in the heart of everyone, there is a desire to make a difference and to be different. That is how God designed us.

Yes, we want to serve you at our church, but we want you to make a difference as well. In chapter 6 we will talk more about this idea of making a difference.

Big adventures for God often begin with small steps. You came to our church for a reason. Perhaps God sent you here so you could make a difference.

You see, we are really glad you are here because you may be here to make a difference beyond any expectations you've ever had.

REASON #4: WE WANT TO GET TO KNOW YOU.

There is really something special when people get to know one another. They learn about their families, their hopes, their dreams, their fears, and their hurts.

You have been a welcomed guest, and you brought your unique self to our church.

Thank you.

But we know there is so much more to learn about you. We know you have stories and insights that will make our congregation a better place. So we hope to get to know you.

Jim was a recent divorcee when he was a guest at church. He obviously was wounded and hurting. He never planned for his marriage to fall apart.

At first, he was hesitant to get involved in the church. He just wasn't sure he was ready to develop relationships at any level. But he got involved, and he started getting to know people. He developed relationships and friendships he never could have anticipated. He loved the people in the church.

But the love was not a one-way street. The people in the church began to know Jim better. And the more they knew about him, the more they liked him. No, Jim was not perfect. Neither were the others in the church. But the more they got to know each other, the more they appreciated each other. They accepted each other just as they were.

We have no doubt we could experience the same with you. We really do want to get to know you. And the more we know you, the more we know we would come to love and appreciate you.

And we think you might feel the same way about the people in our church.

REASON #5: WE LIKE YOU.

So, how can we like someone we don't know, or someone we don't know well (yet)? That's part of the beauty of this church. As we will explain later, we like you because we know God loves you. And because God loves you and me, we are able to connect and appreciate each other just as we are. None of us are the way we want to be.

We like you because we love people the way God loves them: unconditionally. And while we cannot come close to loving others as much as God loves them, we want to show that love as much as possible.

We heard the story of a guest who came to a church with a lot of questions and pain in her life. She did not know what to expect at the church, but any expectations she might have had were quickly met.

"I could tell from the beginning that the people in this church cared for one another," she said. "But I could also tell they weren't a cliquish group not wanting others. They made me feel so welcome. They acted like they really wanted me here."

Her message is our message. We really do want you here. We really like you.

And we really mean it.

WELCOME TO OUR CHURCH

Many years ago, Linda walked into a church not knowing what to expect. There is much to this story, but we will make it brief.

The good news is that she loved the church. She got involved in the church. In fact, to this day, most of her best friends are in the church. She went from a skeptic to a believer and, ultimately, to a highly committed part of her church.

But it did not start that way.

She came to the church with a great amount of uncertainty. She was not even sure why she was visiting that first day.

She also came with expectations that everyone in the church had it all together. She had this unrealistic view that Christians and church members have solved all their problems and don't make any mistakes.

Well, she was wrong. And it took her a while to finally accept that a church is a place for broken people, a place for people who don't have it all together, and a place where everyone is not always nice and happy all the time.

Linda finally came to the realization that church is not a place for perfect people, but a place where broken people come for healing.

Linda's story is our story. Our church is not perfect, far from it. We in the church are not perfect, far from it.

We want you to know you can come to our church just as you are; the rest of us in the church are no better than anyone else.

But we will talk more about this place of imperfect people in the next chapter.

For now, please hear it again: We want you here.

Thank you for taking time to share your life with us. We are here for you, to answer your questions, to pray with you, and just to let you know we care.

We hope the message is clear.

We really want you here.

CHAPTER 2

Do you spend time on Facebook?

There are so many important and positive aspects of this social media tool. I understand why it continues to be a dominant component of our social fabric.

You can connect with family members. You can keep up with old friends from high school or places where you worked together. And, as we are learning more and more, you can get your news at Facebook. Most of the time the news is accurate, but it is not always so. Facebook can't control what every single person posts.

The fastest growing feature on Facebook is video. So now you don't just see words and photos, you can see incredible videos people post. And those videos can be posted live or pre-recorded. It is little wonder Facebook is so incredibly popular.

But there is a downside to Facebook as well. We won't talk about every potential negative feature, but think for a moment about how most people present themselves.

For example, you will make sure you put your best photo on Facebook. When you include your family, it will always be a flattering shot. And you will make sure that all your Facebook friends know when you are visiting some cool place, a place that many may long to go. Your posts will typically let your friends know your family is happy. They will see smiles and fun. They will see us living the good life with good times and good memories.

But they won't see us get into arguments.

They won't see us in some very difficult conflict.

They won't see the inner struggles we experience.

They won't read that we are having trouble paying our bills.

And they won't hear about the meal or vacation that was ruined because our family had a big blow-up.

Sure, there are some exceptions. There are a few people on Facebook who show pain and vulnerability. But the great number of posts shows the good, not the bad; the positive, not the negative; the happy, not the sad; and the victories, not the tragedies. The fact remains: we only disclose what we want people to know about ourselves. We control the message.

So many of us live under the delusion that all Facebook users lead compelling lives. We compare our lives to theirs and think we are really messed up. How have we missed the fun so much of the Facebook world portrays?

We just can't compare. We have missed the mark.

FACEBOOK AND CHURCH AND TOTAL DISCOMFORT

Sometimes we carry the Facebook delusions into our perceptions about churches and those who attend. We think the lives of those church members are near perfect. We think they have their collective acts together.

So how do we feel when we visit a local church? Well, we could feel very uncomfortable, especially if we perceive that our lives cannot compare to the lives of those who attend church.

The story of Frank is a good example of this discomfort. Allow me to go back a few years.

I first met Frank when we he hired me at a bank. I was a student in seminary and needed a way to support my family. He was extremely kind to offer me the job and give me the flexibility I needed to attend classes and spend time with my family.

Frank allowed me to tell him about my beliefs. He was kind when I invited him to church, but he never came. Eventually I graduated from seminary and left the bank. Much to my discredit, I failed to keep up with him over the years.

Fast forward thirty years later. Out of the blue, at least seemingly so, Frank calls me. He wants to get together. He wants to talk about Jesus. And he mentions he is thinking about attending a church.

He also tells me he has a terminal illness.

In one of our times together, I asked Frank why he was so hesitant to attend church. His response was clear and cogent: "Those folks have their acts together. I need to improve some things before I get around them."

Frank was totally honest. He was also totally wrong. I explained to him that those church members have many of the problems, struggles, and bad choices he has. I let them know that none of us are perfect. Frank saw the church from the Facebook perspective.

But soon Frank got it. He started attending church. He soon became a Christian. He saw that the people in the church were normal folks with the same struggles he had. Indeed, he commented often to me how surprised he was to find so many "regular people with regular problems" in the church. In fact, I think he was pretty happy about that reality in a weird kind of way.

When Frank died seventeen months after our reunion, he was a man well loved in the church. He was also a man who finally became comfortable that church was not a place for perfect people.

THE IMPERFECT CHURCH

Local churches got their start in Jerusalem. That was the location of the very first followers of Christ.

Now, we want you to get this picture. Many of these early followers of Jesus saw him die on a cross. Some also saw Jesus alive after he spent three days dead in a tomb. At the very least, they believed some highly credible witnesses who saw his death and resurrection firsthand.

So when the first church began to form, there was great excitement. Many of the early believers sold all their possessions to help others. There was joy. There was unity. There was a commitment to prayer, to fellowship, to meeting together, and to praise. They were so committed that the outsiders looking in were amazed and gave them great favor.

You can read about the beginnings of the first church in Acts 2:42–47. It's a really incredible story. At the very start, it looks like a church that is about as perfect as any group can be.

So how long does this unflawed unity last? Many years? A few years? At least a few months?

How about a few days?

It did not take long before this group of people, many of whom actually saw the resurrected Jesus, began to fuss, feud, and complain. In fact, the Bible records their complaints vividly in Acts 6:1: "In those days, as the disciples were increasing in number, there arose a complaint . . ."

Did you get that?

It only took a few days before this group of dedicated, committed, and life-sacrificing people began to fuss, feud, and complain.

Yep, they started acting like normal people, just like the rest of us.

In fact, the Bible is clear about problems in the early churches. Here are a few examples:

- Immorality among church members (1 Corinthians 5)
- Lawsuits among church members (1 Corinthians 6:1–11)
- Idolatry (1 Corinthians 10:14–22)
- Chaos in church meetings (1 Corinthians 14:26–40)
- Abandonment of the doctrine (Galatians 1:6–10)

- Fights and disagreements among church members (Philippians 4:2–3)
- Temptations toward heresy (Colossians 2:4–23)
- Laziness and slothfulness (2 Thessalonians 3:6–15)
- Divisive behavior (Titus 3:9–11)
- Unforgiving spirit (Philemon 8–22)

Do you get the picture? And remember, these examples came from the first churches in times where there were still witnesses to the resurrection.

Even those churches were not perfect.

And neither is ours.

We have imperfect people in our church. Let me be clear, we are *all* imperfect in our church.

So if you feel like you have baggage and issues and struggles, welcome to the club! Our church is not a perfect place. Our members are not perfect people. If you think in any way, shape, or form you have to "measure up" to be a part of us, throw that illusion away.

We are not a Facebook church with perfect people with no problems and no struggles.

We want you here so you can be a part of a family that has experienced grace and seeks to give grace.

THE IMPERFECT CHURCH AND GRACE

You've probably read or heard this verse in the Bible before. But it never gets old: "For all have sinned and fall short of the glory of God" (Romans 3:23).

If there is any doubt about our imperfections, the Bible addresses it directly. We are all sinners. We are all imperfect. We all have baggage.

But it's the verse that follows that does not get quoted enough. Look at Romans 3:24: "They are justified freely by his grace through the redemption that is in Christ Jesus."

Christians were made right with God (the biblical word is *justified*) because Jesus took the punishment for us by dying on a cross.

We will expand on those thoughts more in chapters 5 and 7. For now, let's look at that word *grace*.

To be clear, we don't take sin lightly. It is an affront to a holy God. Indeed, it separates us from God . . . until we experience grace that reconciles us back to God.

Grace means we receive unmerited favor. It means we get something we don't deserve. It means God loves us so much that he gave his Son to die for us.

So church members are all sinners. We are all imperfect. But a Christian is one who has received forgiveness and the unmerited favor called grace.

SO WHAT?

Why are we telling you this story? First, we want you to be very clear that our church is a church of imperfect people. We, like you, have our challenges, problems, and sins.

Second, we want you to know, as recipients of grace, we want to be dispensers or givers of grace. We won't always get it right, but it is our heartfelt desire to embrace you, to welcome you, and to accept you just as you are.

God gave us that unconditional grace, and that unconditional grace is how we seek to interact with one another. As undeserving recipients of God's love, we seek to show that love to each other . . . and to you.

So, if you were looking for a perfect church with perfect people, you have come to the wrong place. But if you, as an imperfect person and struggler yourself, want to walk alongside other imperfect people, you are indeed at the right place.

Our church is not a place for perfect people.

WE WANT YOU HERE

We want you here to join us in all of our imperfections as we experience grace together.

CHAPTER 3

WE WOULD LIKE TO GET TO KNOW YOU

We were called "balcony dwellers."

I know. It's not a very flattering term. But it brings back incredible memories. It tells the story of when I started going to church as a young married adult. It tells the story of people who decided they would like to get to know strangers to a new community.

My wife and I had been married about a year. I had promised her I would get active in a church. She had grown up in church, but I was a church dropout by age thirteen.

While I did not fulfill my promise to her immediately, I eventually relented and went to church with her.

It was one of the best moves of my life.

The church where we became connected shaped me and changed the path of my life for the better. I found people who were not unlike me. They weren't walking around as paragons of perfection singing, "Holy, Holy, Holy." They were normal people, just like me.

One of the early connections I made was a young men's Bible class. My wife wisely suggested we each attend a like-gender class. She knew I would be more comfortable with a bunch of guys, at least at the onset.

But what was really cool was that these guys really wanted to get to know me better. They were genuine. Sure, each of them had their own struggles. I guess that's why they became such a tight-knit group.

Yes, they really wanted to get to know me.

THE TALE OF THE BALCONY DWELLERS

The Bible study group met right before worship services. The challenge was the growth of the church. They had no room for us to meet. We tried a hallway, but that didn't work. Eventually, we ended up in the balcony of the worship center.

We became the balcony dwellers.

It was in that group that I made friends and connections that would shape my life.

There was Chris, the always-live wire. He never was short on words, a perfect balance for my introverted personality.

Then there was Steve, the steady and encouraging personality. His calm demeanor was sometimes a good antidote to the craziness of some of us.

There was Jim. He was still hurting from a divorce. But, during the pain of this tragedy, he reached out to me. Jim put others before his own very real needs.

Rick was the entrepreneur. He had started a technology components company before most of us knew what technology meant. He would later sell his company and be set for life at a young age.

And you can't forget Lynn. I walked with Lynn through the tragic death of his five-year-old son. That event had a profound effect on my life.

There were several others. And they all reached out.

They made an effort to get to know me. They let me join the balcony dwellers.

A CONNECTED PEOPLE

Think of all the places we connect.

Of course, we are connected to our family, both immediate family and extended family. That is where we make our first connections.

We connect at our places of work. For many of us, we spend more of our waking hours there than any other place.

We connect with our friends, our neighbors, and those merchants we see on a regular basis.

God created us to connect with others. He did not want us to be without human connections. We are indeed a connected people.

We would like to connect with you at our church. Some of the most incredible relationships develop when people get to know each other and discover they have similar beliefs, passions, and goals.

HOW WE CONNECT

We hope you felt a sense of connection when you visited our church. We hope people reached out to you and gave you a handshake or a smile. We hope they made an effort to get to know you.

But we are far from perfect. We don't always connect and greet perfectly. That is why we have different points of connection.

Of course, we try to connect with others in the worship service. We are not merely worshipping God; we are worshipping God with others. There is a profound sense of connection when people come together to worship our Creator.

But we have other places to connect as well. And it's in those other places that some of the most meaningful relationships develop. It includes those who meet in groups, those who serve in ministry, and those who help in a variety of ways.

Let me expand a bit using the balcony dwellers.

The balcony dweller guys connected as we worshipped together. When we were in the worship service, we did not usually sit together, but we saw each other. We looked over as each of us participated in the worship through singing and listening to the message. We indeed did worship God together.

But we connected even more deeply by being in a class together. It was only about fifty minutes a week, but it was a highly meaningful time. And we had a desire to spend time with each other outside of the structure of the class. In fact, Chris and I did some entrepreneurial work together.

Of course, I mentioned Lynn. I was with him when his son died. It was a season of intense grief for him and Elaine, his wife. But it was also a time when our friendship grew even more deeply.

And we all remember profoundly our different ministries in the community, like the time we "adopted" a single mom and her four kids. It was an incredible joy to minister to her and the kids and to help them move toward getting back on their feet.

I'm telling you these stories, because I want you to know we can connect with you on a number of levels. You can ask folks in our church. You can e-mail us. Let us know how you might like to connect even more deeply.

We're serious. We would really like to get to know you.

YOU HAVE SO MUCH TO OFFER

God made you for a purpose. The Bible makes that clear in Ephesians 2:10: "For we are his workmanship, created in Christ Jesus for good works, which God prepared ahead of time for us to do."

You are unique. There is no one like you. You have a purpose in life that is totally unique to you.

WE WOULD LIKE TO GET TO KNOW YOU

So here's what we know for sure. As we get to know you better, we will be richer for it. You will bring something to us that no one else can. God has prepared you for this life even before you were born.

We would love to get to know you and to see the depths of the riches of God's work in your life. We will be better for it.

And we think you will see the blessing of connecting with us as well. That is what is so incredible about churches. Sure, we all have our problems. Sure, we will blow it at times, even with others in the church. But we all are unique creations of God's work, with unique plans developed by God himself.

So it really becomes an incredible reality as more of us join our unique selves for the good works he has prepared us to do.

Can we take the opportunity to get to know you better? Can we begin to explore how you might get to know us better as well? It might be another visit to our worship services. It could be getting involved with one of our groups. Or it might mean trying out involvement in one of our ministries.

You indeed have so much to offer. And we are honored God sent you to our church. For sure, we don't know all of his plans, but we know his plans are good and exciting.

And if God sends you to connect with our church, we know it will be an incredible reality for us to see him work out his plan through your life.

You really have so much to offer. We would be honored to be a part of the journey with you to see it unfold.

WE REALLY WOULD LIKE TO GET TO KNOW YOU

There were many places you could have gone. There were plenty of other choices you could have made.

But you chose to visit us. We are honored. We don't take your choice lightly. In fact, we often see very clearly how God is working in the lives of those he sends our way. And while we don't always see the reasons immediately, it is a joy when you begin to see some of the ways he is working.

Yes, we are honored and blessed you chose to visit us. But we will be even more deeply blessed if we get the opportunity to know you better. Will you let us know if we can help in any way?

So, again, thank you for your presence. It means a lot.

And if we get the opportunity to connect again, we would be honored and thrilled.

We really would like to get to know you.

CHAPTER 4

WHERE FAMILIES GROW STRONG

What is your immediate reaction when you hear the word *family*?

Do you have a sense of warmth, good memories, and pleasant thoughts about the word even today? Perhaps you came from a family where love was evident and demonstrated. You knew your parents cared for you. Your siblings, though not perfect in your mind, have always been fun and supportive.

Perhaps your immediate family today seems like a gift to you. Your spouse is great. Your children are a blessing. *Family* is a good word to you, a word that communicates many positive feelings.

But that is not the case with all of you.

For some of you, family may bring bad memories, pain, or discomfort. Your relationship with your parents was broken. Perhaps you had a marriage that ended in a painful divorce. Or perhaps you struggled with children at young ages or through adulthood.

"Family" typically engenders strong emotions. Some are good. Some are not. Some make you smile. Some cause you to cringe or even cry.

Just like you, our members are experiencing the same things.

Some are married with children at home.

Some are married empty nesters.

Some are never married.

Some are divorced.

Some are widowed.

For each, *family* can mean different things. Family can mean joy. For others . . . well not so much.

Before we share with you about our church family and your family, let us share with you what it means to be a part of God's family. Now that is really exciting!

THE FAMILY OF GOD

God is our Father.

That is one of the most remarkable statements we could ever read. For those who have followed Jesus Christ, God has adopted them as his own. Look at these verses in the Bible from Romans 8:14–16: "For all those led by God's Spirit are God's sons. You did not receive a spirit of slavery to fall back into fear. Instead, you receive the spirit of adoption by whom we cry out, 'Abba, Father!' The Spirit himself testifies with our spirit that we are God's children."

Did you get that? Those who follow Christ are adopted by God! We are a part of God's family. God loves us so much that he wants to have a relationship with us, a family relationship where he is our Father and we are his children.

A young man grasped this reality. He came from an abusive family. His father was an alcoholic, and often lashed out at his family in fits of rage. You can imagine that the young man did not have pleasant thoughts whenever he heard the word *father*. Indeed, any mention of any family relationship brought him pain.

But he spoke of the time when the light went on, when he realized that God wanted to be his Father. The One who created the universe wanted to be his Dad. This Father loved him unconditionally and without hesitation. This Father only wants good things for his children.

To be certain, the pain of his childhood did not go away completely. He still struggles at times with the words *family* or *father*. But now the young man has a new point of reference. He usually thinks of God the Father first. He thinks of God's unconditional love for him. He thinks how he has been adopted into God's family.

THIS CHURCH AS YOUR FAMILY

This church is like a family. We have a lot of loving relationships among those who call this place their church home. For certain, we have imperfect relationships. Like any family, we don't always see eye to eye. We have our moments of disagreement. We have our times of frustration. And we don't always act like a perfect and loving family.

But we are a family. And, in all reality, we love one another.

You have been a guest to our family.

We are grateful.

We welcome you.

THE CHURCH *FOR* YOUR FAMILY

There is a lot of research out there on the relationship between families and those who attend church. We don't want to bore with you with a lot of statistics and data. But look at some of these representative statements about active participation in church for your family members:

Teenagers who attend church are more likely to avoid harmful behavior than their peers according to extensive research.

- Alcohol abuse is much lower.
- They are less likely to smoke cigarettes.
- They are safer behind the wheel.
- They are less prone to violence and criminal behavior
- They have fewer problems in school.
- They are much less likely to sell, buy, or use illegal drugs.

The research, conducted by the University of North Carolina-based National Study of Youth and Religion, showed a positive relationship between religious attendance and higher self-esteem among high school students.

The researchers found that those who attended church were much more likely to enjoy life, to think their lives were useful, to feel hopeful about the future, and to be satisfied with life and enjoy being in school.

Wow.

But the different studies and research have not been limited to just high school age persons. Almost every study out there demonstrates a positive impact upon all family members who attend church. Some point to a longer life span among church attenders. Others note the reduction in levels of depression. And still others show a relationship between healthier marriages and church attendance.

To be transparent, you certainly won't find all of us at our church with perfect lives and perfect families—far from it. Indeed you will find in our church families people who are fellow strugglers. But they have each other. Above all, they worship the one true God who is their Father.

And we realize that the purpose of coming to church is not first to get things fixed in your life. You come to church to worship with others the God who is all-powerful and all-knowing. He is the source of strength. He is the source of comfort. He is the source of healing.

But a commitment to God through the church is healthy for you. It is healthy for your family. It is indeed a place you can call "family."

A PLACE YOU CAN CALL "FAMILY"

You have been a guest to our family. And if God leads you to become a part of our family, we want you to know what it means to have such a powerful relationship with others.

IT MEANS YOU HAVE SOMEONE TO CALL IN TIMES OF NEED

We are here for you. If there is a need in your life or the lives of your loved ones, you can call on us. Recently a church member was rushed to the hospital with a heart attack. While all heart attacks are serious, this one was imminently life-threatening. The wife of the church member was by herself waiting—but only for a few minutes. Fellow members of her church soon surrounded her. She commented very softly but with conviction, "I don't know what I would do without my church family."

A member of the church called upon other fellow members when his son was rebelling. They prayed for him. They were there for him. They comforted him. They were his church family.

IT MEANS YOU HAVE SOMEONE TO ANSWER QUESTIONS

There are no stupid questions at our church. Sometimes life's questions are tough. Sometimes we need help understanding the Bible. And though our church members certainly don't know everything about everything, we can help you find answers to your questions.

Our church is a family. And family members are not ashamed to let other family members know they need help and answers to their questions.

IT MEANS YOU HAVE PEOPLE TO JOIN YOU IN CELEBRATION

Think of some of the celebratory moments of your life. Marriage. The birth of a child. Graduation. Getting a new job. Getting a good medical report. Indeed, there is much to celebrate in this life.

Typically, our friends and family members join us in those celebrations. But it is especially meaningful when those in our church family join us as well. They have walked with us through the good and the difficult times. Their presence means so much during these times of celebration.

IT MEANS YOU WILL BE A SERVING FAMILY MEMBER AS WELL

Let's be clear. There is much you receive when you are a part of a church family. To be certain, the benefits are many. But when you are part of a family, you don't only receive, you give. You don't only get served; you also serve. You don't only receive sacrificial commitments; you give sacrificially to and for others.

Our church is indeed a family. There are times when some family members receive. And there are times when some family members give.

We know you have much to offer. We know you have gifts and abilities. We know God can and does use you greatly. Our church is a family where such gifted people as you both serve and are served.

You are welcome here. And if God leads you to be an ongoing part of our church, we know you will be a gift of service and commitment.

WHERE FAMILIES GROW STRONG

There are all different kinds of families at our church. There are different people at different stages of life. There are families of different sizes, composition, and backgrounds. It is our prayer that our mix of families is a place where all families can grow strong together. Indeed, we are stronger because we are together in this family called the church.

We hope you hear us clearly. You are welcome here. Your family is welcome here. You are welcome here regardless of your background or need. You are welcome here because we are a family that loves to reach out to others.

Please feel free to bring your needs to our family.

Please feel free to bring your questions to our family.

It is our desire not only to say you are welcome here, but to demonstrate that welcome both with our words and our actions.

You are really welcome to our church family.

And you are welcome to find out what it means to be a part of this family.

CHAPTER 5

GETTING TO KNOW THE ONE WHO MADE US

Have you ever met someone famous?

Let me ask it another way.

Have you ever met someone you considered to be a great person? Perhaps meeting him or her was on your bucket list. You are blown away by the opportunity to spend a few minutes with this person, or perhaps get in a photo with them.

Let's assume this person is a famous actor. Maybe you had to wait a few minutes to meet him. You are waiting in a room for him to arrive. As the moment draws closer, you can feel your hands perspiring and your heartbeat increasing. You want to appear calm, but you are failing miserably at your charade. Your mouth is getting dry, and you can feel your knees knocking.

You have your words planned for the moment you meet him. They are perfectly and neatly scripted in your mind.

Then the person arrives.

You reach out your sweaty palms to shake the person's hand. Your well-planned oratory becomes nothing more than a jumble of confused syllables. Your hero looks at you perplexed, smiles, then moves on to the next person.

Ugh.

That didn't work out the way you planned it. But after a few moments of reflection, you are okay. After all, you did get to meet your hero. You did speak for a few moments with the admired person. You even got a photo together.

Despite all the flubs, you met this person. Check one major item off the bucket list. All is well with the world.

Now, think how incredibly awesome it will be to meet God. The Bible teaches us how we will know him, even as he knows us: "For now we see only a reflection as in a mirror, but then face to face. Now I know in part, but then I will know fully as I am fully known" (1 Corinthians 13:12).

But here is the good news. We don't have to wait until we get to heaven to know God. We can get to know him right now.

One of the joys of being part of a church is that you can learn more about God; you can get to know God. And when you are among others in a church, you are getting to know him with others. You are all on the journey together.

WHO IS GOD?

That question is a big question. In fact, it almost seems like it is unanswerable. So what are some of the things we know about God? For starters, here are some of his characteristics.

He is omnipotent. That's a fancy way of saying God is all-powerful. Certainly, if we believe he created everything, we for sure believe he has the power to do anything. And to keep it personal to us, he has the power to take care of anything in our lives. He is all we need.

He is omniscient. That word means, "all-knowing." He knows everything. He knows the past, present, and the future. He knows our thoughts, our needs, our hurts, and our hopes. God is all wise and all knowing.

He is omnipresent. God is everywhere. We cannot contain him. He has no limitations of place or time. On a personal note, God is with us always. Through the Holy Spirit (the third Person of the Trinity), God not only has the ability to be everywhere, he *is* everywhere.

But if we really want to know God, and to know who God is, we simply look to Jesus. In a fascinating exchange with Philip, one of Jesus' disciples, Philip makes this incredible request in John 14:8: "'Lord,' said Philip, 'show us the Father, and that's enough for us.'"

Jesus leaves no doubt of his identity in John 14:9: "Jesus said to him, 'Have I been among you all this time and you do not know me, Philip? The one who has seen me has seen the Father. How can you say, 'Show us the Father'?"

Did you get that? We know who God is by learning who Jesus is. The disciples of Jesus had no need to ask to see the Father, because they had seen him in Jesus. There should have been no doubt. Jesus, the Son, and God, the Father, are one.

You see, we are glad you are here, because together we can learn about and worship Jesus. When we worship him, we are worshipping God. When we learn about Jesus, we are learning about the one true God.

So how do we learn about Jesus at our church? Here are three clear ways you can be a part right now.

LEARNING ABOUT GOD THROUGH THE BIBLE

We are glad you are here.

We are glad you joined us in a worship service. And we hope you learned something about God through the preaching. That is one of the reasons it's so incredible to be a part of our church. We are learning about God through the Bible every single week.

In the Bible, we not only learn about the nature of God and the facts about God, we learn what God has done with us, his creation.

In fact, we learn that God created the heavens and the earth. God created man and woman. God continues to pursue us with love even though we have been disobedient again and again.

But everything in the Bible points to Jesus Christ. You've probably heard the most quoted verse of the Bible, John 3:16: "For God loved the world in this way: He gave his one and only Son, so that everyone who believes in him will not perish but have eternal life."

That is what we are truly learning about God at our church. We are learning how much God loves us. We are learning that God loves us so much he gave his Son to take the punishment for our sins through death on the cross.

We are learning that God wants us on mission today. We are to be telling others what Jesus did for us. And we are learning that Jesus will return one day as well.

There is more. Much more.

Such is the reason we are glad you are our guest. We can all learn together about the God who made us. We can learn about him through the sermons, and the various other ways we study the Bible here.

Thank you for being here. And thank you for joining us as we listen to God's Word preached and taught through the Bible.

LEARNING ABOUT GOD THROUGH CHANGED LIVES

We have tried to make it abundantly clear that we are not perfect, not even close. But you will see something at our church that will point to the power of God. You will see lives that have been changed.

Some of the changes have dramatic stories behind them. Others are more incremental, but no less powerful.

You will learn an inescapable truth getting to know people in our church. God does indeed make a difference in our lives! In fact, you will see that we can learn more about God through these changed lives.

Earlier in this book, we spoke about "the balcony dwellers," a Bible study group in a church many years ago. Just in that one group we could point to a number of changed lives. One of the men, for example, could have been bitter and defeated after he went through a painful divorce. But God took his bitterness away, and he became a joyful person, making a positive difference in the lives of others.

We noted another man who lost his young son due to a heart condition. Again, most of us would be totally defeated after such a tragedy. And though the pain was intense and the grief was deep, God used him to minister to others who experienced tragedies in their lives.

Another of the balcony dwellers became a successful businessman with a successful start-up company. Instead of letting the success and wealth go to his head, he used his gifts to bless others for many, many years.

Such are the type of stories we have among those at this church. We love it when people like you are our guests, because you will have the opportunity to see God working in their lives.

And we realize you have your own story. Perhaps your story is one where God has worked in a great, if not miraculous, way. When you combine your story with those in our church, we all will learn even more about the power and grace of God.

WORSHIPPING THE ONE TRUE GOD

We are glad you are here, because you worshipped God with us. We don't consider our time of worship a routine and perfunctory gathering. We see it as a true opportunity to get to know God better. We understand God more fully and more deeply when we worship him.

We hope you came away from the worship service with a greater sense and awareness of who God is. We hope you sensed His presence in the music and songs. We hope you learned more about His nature in the message that was preached. And we hope you connected with others as we were all connecting with God in the worship services.

Thank you again. It is our prayer you learned a bit more, and got a bit closer, to the God who created us. And should you decide to visit us again, we hope the experience will be even deeper and richer.

GETTING TO KNOW THE ONE WHO MADE US

You have probably heard the classic hymn, "Amazing Grace." You may be able to repeat the first verse from memory:

Amazing grace, how sweet the sound
That saved a wretch like me.
I once was lost, but now am found.
'Twas blind, but now I see.

Those lyrics are a reminder of the great God who created us. He did not have to save us. He did not have to find us. He did not have to give us life.

But he did.

It is truly an amazing grace.

And it is the God of this amazing grace whom we worship at this church. It is that God, the God who created us, about whom we learn a little more each and every week.

Yes, we are glad you are here. But we are glad you are here, because he is here.

And that is what really matters.

CHAPTER 6

COME MAKE A DIFFERENCE WITH US

Have you ever been blown away when you received an unexpected gift? Perhaps you were expecting to receive a gift, but the gift exceeded anything for which you ever dreamed.

You may have been giddy with excitement. Or you may have stood quietly in stunned silence. Or you may have been caught off guard when you noticed the unexpected tears falling down your face.

One of the greatest gifts I ever received was a homemade movie on a DVD (yes, I am dating myself) for my fiftieth birthday. My three sons worked together to produce a collage of photos with a musical background. The songs were about dads, fatherhood, and the great relationships they had with their kids.

As they played the DVD, it hit me. These three sons gave the gift of tribute. They communicated powerfully that I was a good father to them. They showed moments where we, as father and sons, had made memories together.

It was for me. They wanted me to know how much they loved and appreciated their dad.

The moment that thought hit me, I began to sob. I was caught off guard. You might catch me shedding a tear from time to time, but this time I sobbed and cried.

As I tried to sort through my emotions later, I realized why I had been caught off guard emotionally. You see, I was not as great a dad as my sons indicated in their tribute. I had blown it way too many times. Their estimation of me was way too high.

I cried hard because I got a gift I did not deserve.

WITH LOVE, FROM JESUS

Imagine this scene. The greatest person to ever walk this planet was speaking. There was no amplification. If you wanted to hear Jesus then, you had to be quiet and still.

The crowd undoubtedly was hanging on to every word of this miracle worker. His enemies wanted to catch him saying something blasphemous or treasonous. The curious wanted to try to make sense of who this man really was. And his followers wanted to soak in every word, for they knew Jesus was more than a man.

Jesus spoke in parables and illustrations. At this point, he contrasts himself with those who wish evil on others. "A thief," he says, "comes to steal and kill and destroy." The words are harsh but clear. Steal. Kill. Destroy.

And then Jesus speaks in contrast with his own mission. "I have come so that they may have life and have it abundance" (John 10:10).

Do you see the contrast? On the one hand it's steal, kill, and destroy. On the other hand, Jesus says life and abundance.

I wonder if anyone listening to Jesus began to weep, perhaps as I did when my sons played the DVD. I wonder if they realized the import and the meaning of what Jesus just said. He had come not only to give life, but to give it in abundance. The word that Jesus used for "abundance" has the meaning of something that exceeds any expectation we have.

Yes. When we grasp what Jesus was saying, we have to be blown away. Jesus is offering us not only eternal life; he is offering us a life that is abundant, beyond any expectations we could imagine.

You see, you were not meant to have a normal life, whatever that means. You were meant to have an abundant life. You were created to be different and to make a difference. You were not meant to live the same, lame, tame life most people live.

Such is the power of the abundant life. Jesus provides for you a life that is different and makes a difference.

Did you get that? You were made to make a difference.

COME SERVE WITH US

Most of the time when you are a guest, the role of the host is to serve you. To be clear, we want to serve you here. We want to be a place where you can bring your needs and your burdens. Without a doubt, we want to serve you at our church.

But we also invite you to serve with us. You see, when you really make a difference, it's because you are looking beyond yourself to the needs of others.

When you come to our church, you have the opportunity to serve others in the congregation, from the youngest child to the senior saint in a retirement home. You get to make a difference in people's lives. As a result, you become different.

When Jesus talked about the abundant life, he paid the ultimate cost for us to have that life. He died on a cross to take away our sins and to give us the promise of eternal life. He is the greatest difference maker, and he demonstrated that reality by giving his life for us.

When you come to our church, you will be a difference maker. And as you begin by seeing fellow church members serve one another, you will be excited about serving alongside them.

But we don't just serve each other at our church, we serve those outside our church. And we invite you to make a difference by serving with us.

A church in south Florida was struggling. Not many guests showed up each week. The members were frustrated and discouraged. It was not a joyous time at the church.

Then the pastor began to talk to many of the members about the challenges. What he heard was not what he expected. One of the questions he asked each of those members was, "When our church was really a great place to be, what was taking place?"

He expected them to talk about a certain attendance level or the implementation of some of their favorite programs. But that's not what the people told him. Let me try my best to re-create a conversation the pastor had with one of the church members, a conversation reflecting most of those interviewed.

"Pastor," the seventy-four-year-old woman began, "it's really easy to pinpoint the days when I was most excited about this church. It was when I could walk downtown, and I would hear from people outside the church say how much the ministry of our church meant to them. Our focus was on the community. Our focus was on the schools, and the hurting, and those who were not followers of Christ. So much of what we were doing was outside the walls of our church."

The pastor stopped her. "Say that last sentence again," he said. And so she repeated it. "So much of what we were doing was outside the walls of our church."

That is it, he thought. *That's what is missing here.*

So the church began focusing more and more of their efforts and ministries on "the others" instead of themselves alone. They then began to make a difference, a big difference.

That is the heartbeat of our church. We want to make a difference outside the walls of our church. We want to be difference makers.

We invite you to join us on this mission. We invite you to come serve with us.

We invite you to be a difference maker with us.

COME GO WITH US

This whole idea of serving others is really about going. It's about going outside of the walls of our church to make a difference.

Before Jesus left his followers for good, he gave final instructions—called the Great Commission. In fact, immediately before he left his followers, Jesus said these words in Acts 1:8: "But you will receive power when the Holy Spirit has come on you, and you will be my witness in Jerusalem, in all Judea and Samaria, and to the end of the earth."

And that was it. Jesus left.

The Bible records it this way: "After he had said this, he was taken up as they were watching, and a cloud took him out of their sight" (Acts 1:9).

The last words Jesus said could be summarized in one word: Go.

Perhaps the best known Great Commission passage is Matthew 28:19–20: "Go, therefore, and make disciples of all nations, baptizing them in the name of the Father and of the Son and of the Holy Spirit, teaching them to observe everything I have commanded you. And, remember, I am with you always, to the end of the age."

Another way to translate that passage would be to begin with these words: "As you are going . . ." In other words, God wants us on mission. God wants us to go. God wants us to make a difference.

You are welcome here. And we hope you will go with us into our community and beyond to make a difference. That is what God wants us to do. So that is what we do.

TO MAKE A DIFFERENCE

We are always so excited when guests visit our church. We get excited about you being here. We get excited about serving you. And we get excited about you serving alongside us making a difference.

The Bible teaches us to live like Christ did, but sometimes we may not know exactly what that means. While there are many passages in the Bible that point us in the right direction, these verses from Philippians 2:5–7 make it very clear: "Adopt the same attitude as that of Christ Jesus, who existing in the form of God, did not consider equality with God as something to be exploited. Instead he emptied himself by assuming the form of a servant."

Wow! Let those words soak in for a moment. We are to be like Christ. We are to be like Jesus who, even though he is God, took on the form of a servant while he lived on earth.

There it is. There is where true fulfillment is found. If we are to make a difference in this life, we are to serve others. After all, that is exactly what Jesus did.

Thank you for being our guest. Thank you for honoring us with your presence. We are glad you are here.

And we pray that we may not only get to see you again but, perhaps, we can even serve together in the near future.

Thank you so much for being here. And hear our invitation to go serve with us.

That's what it means to follow the example of Christ.

That's what it means to make a difference.

CHAPTER 7

THANK YOU FOR BEING HERE

Steve Schaufele is from Okotoks, a town in the province of Alberta, Canada. It is situated on the Sheep River, approximately eleven miles south of Calgary.

Steve and his wife, Jesse, have four children. Now here is the most fascinating fact about Steve. Nobody has ever met anyone who knows Steve who does not like him—really like him. In fact, most people speak effusively when they speak of Steve. Rarely does a person generate such a positive response from people.

One of Steve's favorite phrases is "Fantastic!" or "That is fantastic!" He has an unbridled enthusiasm for life and for people. When you are around Steve, you feel special because, well, he really believes you are special.

He said something etched in my memory. Without any pretense, but with all sincerity, Steve said, "I am so grateful for you."

Nothing more. Nothing less. Just six words that meant the world.

He didn't have to say it. But he did. And he really meant it.

We hope you sensed that same sentiment when you visited our church. We hope you sensed how grateful we are for you. We hope you grasp that we mean it when we say, "We are so grateful for you."

You didn't have to come to our church. But you did.

You didn't have to take time from your schedule to be a part of our lives. But you did.

You didn't have to come to a place where perhaps you knew very little. But you did.

Thank you.

And please hear these words with the same sincerity Steve spoke them to me, "We are so grateful for you."

WE ARE GRATEFUL BECAUSE GOD CAN WORK THROUGH YOU

Paul was an apostle who traveled many places to start churches and to encourage existing churches in the first century AD. One of his favorite churches was in Philippi in the Roman Empire. Listen to his words of encouragement in Philippians 1:3–6:

"I give thanks to my God for every remembrance of you, always praying with joy for all of you in my every prayer, because of your partnership in the gospel from the first day until now. I am sure of this, that he who started a good work in you will carry on to completion until the day of Christ Jesus."

Did you get that? Look at that last sentence one more time: "I am sure of this, that he who started a good work in you will carry on to completion until the day of Christ Jesus."

Paul was clear. God had started something in the lives of those early Christians, and he would carry his purpose and plan to completion. But that key sentence may raise the question: How does he start the good work in me anyway?

And that, my friend, is a great question.

Here is the simple but most profound response, straight from the Bible.

First, we are all sinners. We have all messed up. None of us is perfect. The Bible says in Romans 3:23: "For all have sinned and fall short of the glory of God." The Bible does not mince words. We cannot be with God in heaven if we have unforgiven sins. We cannot enter his presence because we have sinned.

But God is a loving and forgiving God. He provided a way for our sins to be taken away. He provided total and complete forgiveness. Though we deserve to be punished for our sins, he sent his Son, Jesus, to take the punishment for us.

Why? Why was God willing and even desiring to send His own Son to die for us? The Bible is crystal clear here. It's probably the best-known verse in Scripture, John 3:16: "For God loved the world this way: He gave his one and only Son, so that everyone who believes in him will not perish but have eternal life."

Do you grasp this reality? God loves us so much that he sent his Son Jesus to take the punishment for our sins. That is the simple, profound, and total truth of it all. God made that sacrifice because he loves us.

But also note the little phrase "everyone who believes in him." This offer of God's love, God's salvation, and God's forgiveness is for those who believe in him. But don't confuse that word *believe* with a mere acknowledgment of God's existence. It means we trust God for everything he says.

We trust him for forgiveness because we know we have sinned and need forgiveness. We therefore repent, or turn from sin. When we say we need to repent, we are not only acknowledging we need forgiveness for our sins, we desire actively to turn away from those sins.

Look at these words in Acts 3:19: "Therefore repent and turn back, so that your sins may be wiped out." It's simple but profound. If we truly repent, God removes our sins from our lives. We are clean and pure before him.

As you ponder these words, remember, it's God who is moving in your life. It is God who is the source of our salvation. It is God who gives us this unmerited and undeserved gift. It is not by any of our own works: "For you are saved by grace through faith, and this is not from yourselves; it is God's gift not from works, so that no one can boast" (Ephesians 2:8–9).

Yes, you are welcome here. But even more, you are welcome in the presence of God. Have you truly repented from sins and placed your faith in Jesus Christ? We welcome you here. And God welcomes you so he can complete the work he started when you accepted his Son as your Lord and Savior.

THANK YOU FOR LETTING US SERVE YOU AND SERVE WITH YOU

We would welcome the opportunity to talk to you about Jesus and what he offers you and me. We would love to talk with you about ways we can serve you and pray for you. We would love to talk with you about serving alongside us, as we look at the possibility of you serving others in our church.

When you put this brief book down, consider contacting us. Perhaps you could call us or e-mail us. Perhaps we could get together for coffee and get to know each other better. Perhaps you have some questions after visiting with us. Perhaps you have questions after reading this book. Perhaps you have questions about our church.

Please know that we desire to serve you. We desire to know you better. We desire to answer any questions we may have.

Please contact us. Let us know how we can help. You are truly welcome here. We truly want you here.

YOUR VISIT WAS NO ACCIDENT

His name is Tim. Many years ago he visited a church. It was the first time in his adult life he had been in a church. He had memories of his childhood church, but he stopped attending when he was fourteen years old.

So when he visited the church, he admittedly was intimidated and uncertain. Indeed, he had second thoughts about walking in the church building after he arrived in the parking lot.

Then something happened.

He's not sure it was just one thing, but many.

He saw people smiling. He saw people smiling at him. And when he entered the doors of the church building, he experienced warm greetings and kind words.

Once he settled in his chair for the worship services, he sensed something different. People were truly worshipping God. He saw it in the songs they sang, in the way they listened to the preacher, and in the ways they prayed together.

Tim returned. And he returned again.

Tim would soon become a Christian, a follower of Christ. He started living, not out of guilt and obligation but out of joy and desire, as a selfless person serving others. His struggling business turned around. He was surprised. He made no bargains with God. But God seemed to bless his business as he desired to serve God more.

Tim would become a highly successful businessman. Many of the profits of his company were used to help underprivileged children in his community. He made a huge difference in his church, in his community, and in the world.

Reflecting back on that day he first visited the church, Tim shared these words: "It was no accident I went to church that day. God had plans so far beyond my own dreams. It was his plans. It was no accident."

And it is no accident you visited our church. We can't know right now how God will take this visit and use you. But we know there was a reason he brought you to us. We know he has plans for you.

BY THE WAY, WE AREN'T PERFECT!

Though we don't have to tell you again, we are not a perfect church. We are a church of fellow strugglers. We don't always do the right thing or say the right thing.

But, despite our struggles and mistakes, we still love our God and love each other. That is what we hope you noticed when you visited our church. We hope you notice a lot of love, a lot of smiles, and a lot of joy. And we hope you noticed that some of that love, that joy, and those smiles were directed at you.

We really are glad you are here.

THANK YOU FOR BEING HERE

You have given so much. You have given us your time. You have given us your presence. And you have even given us the honor of reading this little book we gave you.

I know we have been redundant in our gratitude for thanking you for visiting with us. But we really want you to hear again and again how much your visit means to us.

And we mean it. Let us know how we can serve you. Let us know of any questions you may have. Please let us know. Call us. E-mail us. Contact us. We are ready and willing to serve however we can.

God brought you here to be our guest. We don't take that reality for granted. And it is our hope and prayer that we will have another opportunity to see you and to get to know you better.

Thank you for being our guest.

Thank you for your time.

Thank you for your presence.

And in case we have not made it very, very, clear, let us end with these brief words.

We want you here.